Creative Ideas

Program Authors

Connie Juel, Ph.D.

Jeanne R. Paratore, Ed.D.

Deborah Simmons, Ph.D.

Sharon Vaughn, Ph.D.

ISBN 0-328-21458-2
Copyright © 2008 Pearson Education, Inc.

9 10 V011 12 11 10 09 08
CC1

PEARSON
Scott Foresman

Editorial Offices: Glenview, Illinois • Parsippany, New Jersey • New York, New York
Sales Offices: Boston, Massachusetts • Duluth, Georgia • Glenview, Illinois
Coppell, Texas • Sacramento, California • Mesa, Arizona

UNIT 3 Contents

Creative Ideas

Contents

Ideas Become Inventions

See page 27 for My New Words!

Ideas Become Inventions

What can you do with an idea? You can plan and make an invention! Inventions help us and make things fun. Some are huge, like jets. Some are not huge, like gum and notes that stick.

6

What is the sign of a good invention? This man had an idea. His name was Alexander Graham Bell. Alexander Graham Bell made this machine. It helped us. It let us chat with pals. Kids still use it to chat with pals.

Kids can make things too. A kid named Frank had a drink. It had a stick in it. Frank took his drink out of his house in winter and left it.

Time passed, and his drink froze with the stick in it. It was like an ice cube on a stick.

Frank had made a snack on a stick. Kids still like these snacks on sticks. Kids like grape ice snacks. Kids like lime ice snacks. Yum, yum!

Eve thinks and thinks. Then Eve plans and plans. Next, Eve takes tubes, tape, and wire to make an invention. Eve's best pal, Suze, will help Eve.

"We can use this at camp!" Suze tells Eve. What do you think these best pals will make? What can you make? What is the sign of a good invention?

IN-LINE

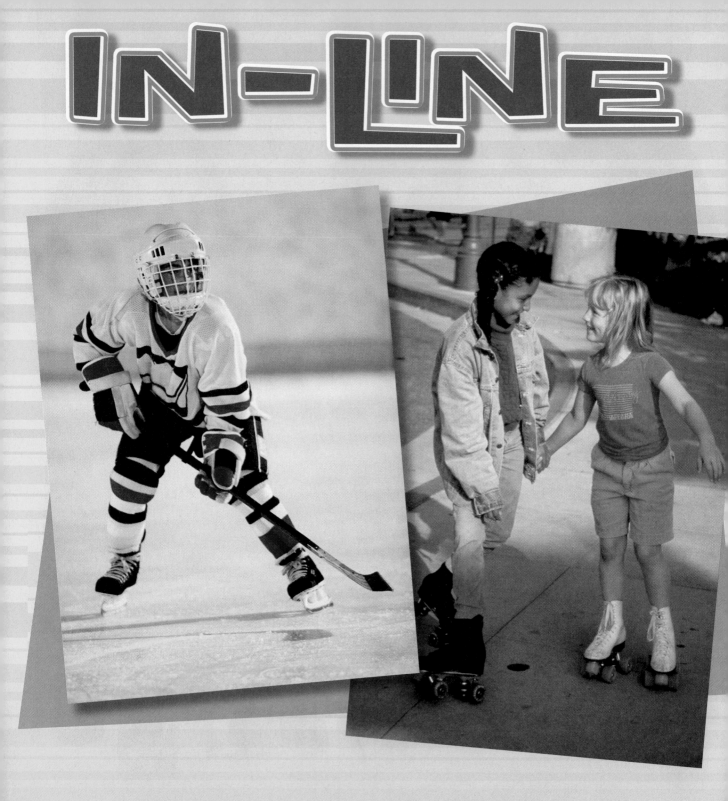

It's lots and lots of fun to skate! Ice skates use long blades and zip fast on white ice. Kids can skate on places that aren't ice too. Then kids don't use skates with blades. These skates use wheels.

SKATES

by Carla Smith

This is an in-line skate. The idea for it came from Scott and Brennan Olson. The Olsons spotted an old, odd skate in a shop. It had wheels in a long line. This odd skate gave these men an idea.

Brennan Olson

Scott Olson

Back at their house, the Olsons took blades off ice skates. They added a long line of wheels on one skate and then on the other. Next, the men added brakes to help the skates stop.

brake

These skates went fast. And brakes helped make them safe. Little kids liked them. Big kids liked them. Moms and dads liked them!

The men grinned, "We can make lots of in-line skates and sell them!"

The men got a machine that helped them
make in-line skates. They made the skates at
home. People kept asking for skates. The men
had to hire help. The big sales of in-line skates
are a sign that these men did a good job.

My New Words

house*

A **house** is a building where people live.

idea*

An **idea** is a thought or plan.

invention

An **invention** is a new thing that someone thinks of and makes.

machine*

A **machine** is something with moving parts that does work for you.

sign*

A **sign** has pictures or words that tell you something important. A **sign** can also tell of something to come or something to look for.

*tested high-frequency words

Contents

WAYS TO COMMUNICATE

See page 53 for My New Words!

29

WAYS TO COMMUNICATE

Kids can communicate with pals in lots of ways. Kids can get together and chat. And they can chat when they are not close. Kids can use this machine to chat. Ring, ring!

Kids can use this machine to chat. One kid hits his switch and chats. Then his buddy can press her switch and chat back. Chatting like this is fun! Would you like to try it?

Kids can communicate with notes. Kids can
jot quick notes and hand them to pals.

Kids can send quick notes on machines too.
Pals get these notes fast!

Kids can also send notes by adding stamps and dropping them in a box. Trucks pick up these notes. Planes can take notes and fly them to other lands. Have you found notes in your box?

Some kids must communicate with their hands. This kid made a sign with his hands that stood for "happy."

His buddy will use his hands and make signs back. These kids can have fun chatting this way.

Not just kids communicate. Hens cluck. Ducks quack. Some bugs can make songs by rubbing one back leg against another. Wild cats can hiss if they are mad. And when a puppy is happy, you can tell!

Dots
and
Dashes

by Aaron Lewis

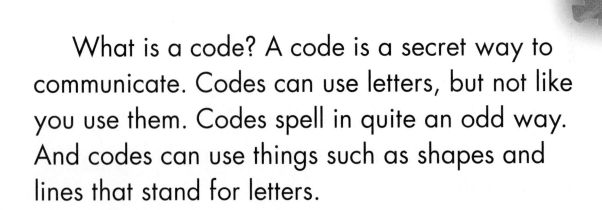

What is a code? A code is a secret way to communicate. Codes can use letters, but not like you use them. Codes spell in quite an odd way. And codes can use things such as shapes and lines that stand for letters.

People can communicate with codes if they know what those lines and shapes stand for. Sending notes in code is like sending secrets.

This man is Samuel Morse. Samuel liked making codes. He made an odd code that used dots and dashes. These dots and dashes stood for letters.

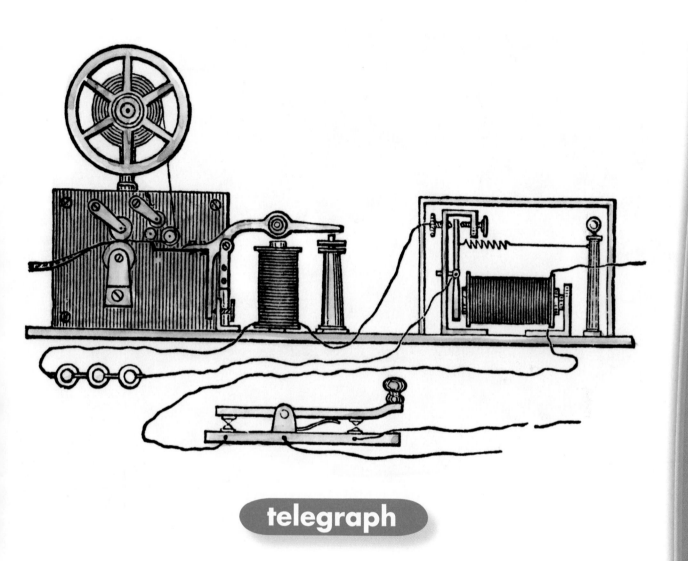

telegraph

This is a machine that Samuel made. He made it for sending his code. It had lots of switches and presses. It had long, skinny wires that rested against other long, skinny wires.

Samuel and his buddies tried sending notes by using his code. They tapped and tapped. They tapped long for dashes. They tapped fast for dots. Dash, dash, dot, dot, dash, dot, dot, dot.

Tap! Tap! Click! The code was sent through skinny wires to men miles and miles away. Click! Tap! Click!

These men jotted dots and dashes on note pads. They could tell what the dashes and dots stood for.

People in Samuel's time could not just chat with buddies miles and miles away. They could not send letters fast. Did Samuel's code help? Yes, it did.

A	. _	S	. . .
B	_ . . .	T	_
C	_ . _ .	U	. . _
D	_ . .	V	. . . _
E	.	W	. _ _
F	. . _ .	X	_ . . _
G	_ _ .	Y	_ . _ _
H	. . . .	Z	_ _ . .
I	. .	1	. _ _ _ _
J	. _ _ _	2	. . _ _ _
K	_ . _	3	. . . _ _
L	. _ . .	4	. . . . _
M	_ _	5	. . . . .
N	_ .	6	_ . . . .
O	_ _ _	7	_ _ . . .
P	. _ _ .	8	_ _ _ . .
Q	_ _ . _	9	_ _ _ _ .
R	. _ .	0	_ _ _ _ _

Samuel Morse had a wild idea that helped people communicate. Samuel had found a way to send notes fast by using a code. His code is still used. It is named Morse code.

Gramps Learns New Things

by Roberto Marcos
illustrated by Elizabeth Allen

"Andy, Gramps is flying in to see us! He will get here by lunch," smiled Mom.

Andy grinned. Andy liked chatting with Gramps and telling him about his classes and his buddies.

At last Gramps rang the bell. He gave Mom and Andy big hugs. Mom smiled, "Andy misses you lots! It makes us happy when you are with us." "I bet Andy has lots to tell!" Gramps smiled.

Andy grinned. He did have lots to tell Gramps!
Andy just got a computer. It stood on his desk
against Mom's shelf in the den.

"My, that's a fancy one," said Gramps. "Look at
those switches! Get my glasses. I will take a look."

"You can use this computer to send notes to buddies," said Andy.

"You can send notes with this?" asked Gramps.

"Yes," grinned Andy. "And then you can get notes back!"

"Why not try it?" smiled Andy.

Gramps tried and tried but could not send notes. At last Gramps cried, "I just can't use this silly thing!"

So Andy sat by Gramps and helped.

Gramps smiled and sent a note to his buddy.

"This is fun," smiled Gramps. "But can I use this computer for other things?"

"You can use it to get on the Web. That's how you can learn lots," Andy told him. "Let's try it."

Gramps found funny jokes and names of wild plants. He checked maps. "It is sunny and dry in this place!" said Gramps.

Gramps grinned. "It is fun to try new things. I learned lots from you, Andy. Thanks!"

When Gramps got home, he sent this note:

Andy, I got a computer. I used it and sent this note. This is fun, isn't it? I will like sending and getting notes!

Andy grinned. Now he and Gramps can chat all the time!

What a Smart Idea!

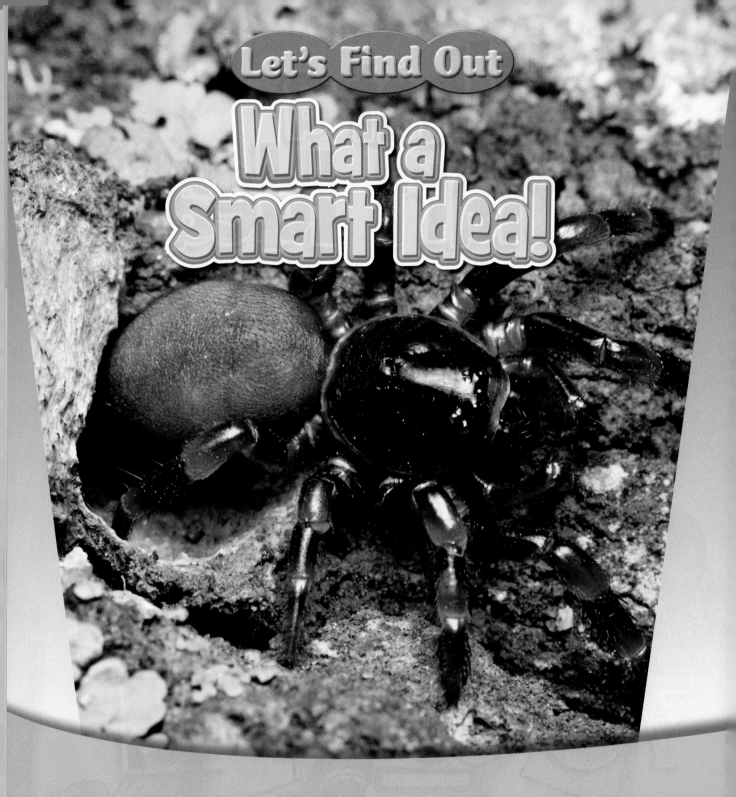

This big spider is smart. It made a trap to get a snack. It mixed thick mud and silk to make its trap. Then it placed twigs and bits of bark on top. That made the trap hard to spot.

A fat frog hopped in front of the trap. It didn't spot the trap. The big spider jumped up and grabbed the frog.

Munch, munch! This frog will become a yummy snack.

This chimp likes bugs as snacks. But it's hard to get bugs. The chimp can try. But bugs hide in a big nest. And the chimp's arm just isn't long enough.

This chimp is smart. It picked up a long, sharp stick. It poked that stick far up in the nest. Bugs hopped on it and the chimp grabbed it back.

Munch, munch! These bugs will become a yummy snack.

A man thought fish would make a fine snack.
But this man didn't have a pole. He didn't even
have a stick. And the fish were swimming far
from the dock. What if the man used a net?

The man picked up his big net and dipped it in the water. Six quick fish swam past. But one fish got stuck. The man grabbed his net and lifted it up. Munch, munch! This fish will become a yummy snack.

A kid went to an apple farm. She hoped
to pick ripe, red apples as her snack. But they
were far up in the top branches.

The kid thought long and hard. At last she grabbed a long stick and poked at the branches. Five big, ripe apples dropped. Munch, munch! These red apples will become a yummy snack.

A Nutty Story

by Consuela Sparks
illustrated by Laura Jacobsen

Crows are big, black birds. Crows can fly. Crows like to munch on things that come in shells, such as clams and nuts.

Are crows born smart? Can they even think or plan? Crows can't tell us. We must try to see.

People spotted crows dropping clams on rocks at the shore. But why? The clam shells cracked against hard rocks. The crows split those clam shells. Now the crows had clams to munch!

Crows must have thought this plan was good with nuts too. But nuts did not split. Crows came up with this new plan.

Lots of people stood as cars went past. A black crow sat on grass by them. It had six big nuts.

Cars went past. Horns honked. Tires spun. At last the cars stopped on the white line.

People crossed. The black crow grabbed nuts and made five short hops. Then it stopped. It didn't plan on crossing. It was fixing its lunch.

The crow dropped nuts in front of cars. Then it made five short hops back. Cars started up and went fast. While the crow sat on grass, cars drove on nuts and cracked them!

The crow hopped back when cars stopped again. It grabbed the cracked nuts that had become its lunch. Then it went on the grass and ate those nuts. Yum, yum! Crows ARE smart!

Think Smart!

by Carla Robbins
illustrated by Laura Freeman-Hines

School had ended. It was hot. Mark, Norm, and Barb sat on the shore. Fish swam back and forth in front of them.

"This is a bore," said Norm. "What can we do today?"

"Let's catch these big fish," said Barb. "If only we had fishing poles!"

"Let's use nets," stated Norm.

"What sort of idea is THAT?" asked Mark. "We don't even have nets."

"Well, we could make a thing that is LIKE a net," said Barb. "Let's think up lots of ideas and then form a plan."

"But Mark thinks my ideas are just silly!"
Norm cried.

"Even plans that start silly can become
smart," Barb stated.

"Let's list our ideas, starting with mine!"
grinned Norm.

Barb smiled and got her note pad.

Norm said, "Let's catch fish with Mom's scarf."
Barb added, "Let's catch fish with sharp twigs."
Barb jotted lots of ideas. Then she stopped.
"These ideas are not bad," Barb said, "but we
must think of more."

Mark asked if hats with big brims could catch fish. The kids thought. Then Mark cried, "I know a plan to try!"

Mark grabbed the hat that Barb had on.

He used the string to put Barb's hat on a branch. Mark had made this thing to catch fish! It had a pole. It was LIKE a net. The kids went fishing.

A big fish swam by. Barb tugged on the branch and lifted her big hat. She had the fish!

Then Norm and Mark got more fish. Soon six big fish flopped on shore.

"Let's take them home and ask Mom to bake them for lunch," stated Barb.

Mark, Norm, and Barb ate yummy fish in their yard.

"Mark's plan was smart," grinned Barb.

"It wasn't just my plan," stated Mark. "Your ideas helped me think up that smart plan."

"They did?" smiled Barb.

Mark smiled back. "Your ideas made ME start thinking!"

I Built a Fabulous Machine

by Jack Prelutsky

Read Together

I built a fabulous machine
to keep my room completely clean.
It swept it up in nothing flat—
has anybody seen the cat?

My New Words

become*   It has **become** warmer.

brim   A **brim** is a wide edge that sticks out from around a hat.

crow   A **crow** is a large, shiny, black bird with a loud cry.

even*   **Even** though it was hot, she wore a jacket. Do you **even** know that boy you waved to?

front*   The **front** part of something is the part that faces forward. The **front** of something is also the first part or the beginning.

spider   A **spider** is very small and has eight legs.

thought*   A **thought** is something that a person thinks.

*tested high-frequency words

Contents

Figure It Out

See page 113 for My New Words!

Figure It Out

Can kids think smart? Kids can.

At home, some things are hard to get to. This kid can't get to the sink. What can kids do about this problem?

Kids can just step up. But it's easy to slip. Kids must hang on as they step up and step down.

These kids will have a party. Kids will invite their pals. Kids make cards that tell the time and place of the party. Kids make maps on the cards and write, "Follow this map for fun!"

It is time to send the cards. But these kids have a problem. They do not have stamps.

As usual, these kids think smart. These kids will TAKE the cards to their pals!

Pet dogs must get fed and brushed. They must go out too. But big dogs can tug hard and escape. If that happens, it's a big problem!

This kid knew that it takes more than one kid to take a huge dog out. He asked his pal for help. If the dog tugs hard, both kids just tug back. This dog can't run off!

Can kids think smart? Kids can!

Justin's Bikes for Kids

by Becca Case

illustrated by Joel Spector

Justin liked riding racing bikes. He also liked fixing them.

Justin spotted an old bike. He fixed it up like new. Fixing bikes was easy and fun for Justin.

Justin rode his fixed-up bike. It was not a racing bike. Justin didn't like it as much as the usual racing bike he rode.

Then he fixed up one more bike. Justin still liked his racing bike more. But he DID like fixing bikes! This gave Justin an idea.

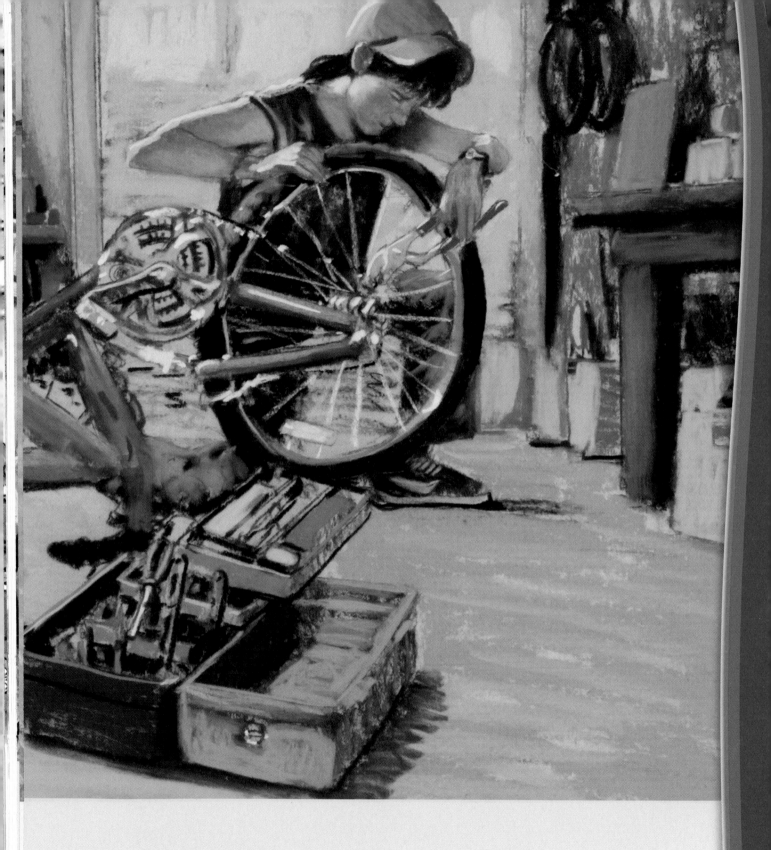

Justin knew a place to take his fixed-up bikes. Kids who did not have moms or dads lived at this place. Justin gave these kids his bikes.

A smart idea can start with just a guess. Then it gets tested to tell if it is correct or not.

If a guess isn't correct, that's OK. Tests help us. They make us think about what to try next.

Smart ideas can take lots of testing. That can take time, but it'll let us end up with smart answers!

Fun Party Ideas
1. tag
2. egg toss
3. make crafts
4. sing
5. share cake
6. water balloons
7. give gifts

Kids can help kids get ideas. Take time to trade ideas with a pal. You'll both think up lots of fun things. Make a nice, long list. Pick the best things and try them.

It's fine to get ideas from artists. Just don't forget to invent your art ideas too.

Artists use colors, along with shapes, in art. When you admire art, think about its colors and shapes. You can get the best ideas. Just think!

Beautiful IDEAS

by Josie Abrams

Fine artists get ideas for art in many places. Artist Mary Cassatt didn't have kids, but she got along well with them.

Children on the Beach, 1884, Mary Cassatt.

Spending time with both kids and moms helped her get ideas for her art.

In Mary Cassatt's art, moms hug kids. Girls sit by the shore, and kids run in gardens.

Claude Monet had huge gardens filled with bursts of color. This artist liked standing and gazing at his fine gardens.

The Japanese Bridge, Giverny, 1892, Claude Monet.

Can you guess where Claude Monet got ideas for his art? Yes! When you see his art, you'll think that you are standing in his fine garden with him.

When artist Rufino Tamayo was a kid, he helped sell fresh plums and limes. He helped sell fresh corn, garlic, and peppers too.

Still Life of Watermelon and Plums, 1941, Rufino Tamayo.

Later, Rufino Tamayo made pictures of these yummy things in his art.

This artist used his brush to make swirls and curls of color that shimmer and shine.

Clementine Hunter didn't make her first art until she was past fifty. Things around her gave her ideas. She put gardens and churches in her art.

The Wash, 1950s, Clementine Hunter.

YELP!
HELP!

by Gloria Vallejo

illustrated by Rémy Simard

My New Words

admire When you **admire** something, you look at it with pleasure.

along* Trees are planted **along** the street.
We took our dog **along**.
I get **along** well with him.

artist An **artist** is a person who makes art.

both* **Both** houses are pink.
Both belong to her.

color* A **color** is either red, yellow, blue, or any of these mixed together.

elf In stories, an **elf** is a tiny make-believe person.

guess* A **guess** is an idea you have when you are not sure of something.

plenty **Plenty** is all that you need.
You have **plenty** of time.

*tested high-frequency words

Acknowledgments

Text

82 "I Built a Fabulous Machine" from *It's Raining Pigs & Noodles* by Jack Prelutsky. Text copyright © 2000 by Jack Prelutsky. Used by permission of HarperCollins Publishers.

Illustrations

4–5, 18–25 Bill McGuire; **29, 44–51** Elizabeth Allen; **55, 70–81** Laura Freeman-Hines; **55, 64–69** Laura Jacobsen; **82** Jeff Shelly; **84–85, 92–99** Joel Spector; **86–91** Gary LaCoste; **100–110** Jackie Urbanovic; **115, 130, 132–140** Remy Simard

Photographs

Every effort has been made to secure permission and provide appropriate credit for photographic material. The publisher deeply regrets any omission and pledges to correct errors called to its attention in subsequent editions.

Unless otherwise acknowledged, all photographs are the property of Scott Foresman, a division of Pearson Education.

Photo locators denoted as follows: Top (T), Center (C), Bottom (B), Left (L), Right (R), Background (Bkgd).

Opener: ©Blend Images/Getty Images, **1** ©Blend Images/Getty Images; **3** (T) ©DK Images, (TC) Lindsey Stock/©DK Images, (BR) Corbis; **6** (T) ©Bettmann/Corbis, (CL) ©Akhtar Soomro/Corbis; **7** (CL) ©DK Images, (CR) Lindsey Stock/©DK Images, (T) Corbis; **8** ©DK Images; **9** ©ImageState; **12** (CR) ©Myrleen Ferguson Cate/PhotoEdit, (CL) ©William Sallaz/Duomo/Corbis; **14** (CL, CR) ©Rollerblade USA Corp.; **15** ©Charlie Borland/Index Open; **16** ©Charlie Borland/Index Open; **17** ©Lori Adamski Peek/Getty Images; **26** (T) Dave King/©DK Images, (TR) ©photolibrary/Index Open, (CR) Andy Crawford/©DK Images, (CR) ©DK Images, (BR) ©FogStock/Index Open; **28** ©Blend Images/Getty Images; **30** Getty Images; **31** ©Tony Freeman/ PhotoEdit; **32** ©Blend Images/Getty Images; **33** ©Tony Freeman/PhotoEdit; **35** ©Myrleen Ferguson Cate/PhotoEdit; **38** The Granger Collection, NY; **39** North Wind Picture Archives; **40** The Granger Collection, NY; **41** North Wind Picture Archives; **42** North Wind Picture Archives; **43** ©DK Images; **56** ©Anthony Bannister/Corbis; **57** Getty Images; **58** Getty Images; **59** ©Steve Bloom Images/Alamy Images; **60** ©Dennis Frates/Alamy Images; **61** ©Colinspics/Alamy Images; **62** ©James Lauritz/ Alamy Images; **63** ©Michael Newman/PhotoEdit; **64** Getty Images; **66** Getty Images; **69** Getty Images; **85** ©Pat Doyle/Corbis; **112** (TR, BR) ©Pat Doyle/Corbis, (CR) ©Royalty-Free/Corbis; **114** ©Juan Silva/Getty Images; **117** ©Michael Goldman/ Getty Images; **118** ©Richard T. Nowitz; **121** (CL) ©Royalty-Free/Corbis, (TC) ©Juan Silva/Getty Images; **122** (C) ©Bettmann/Corbis, (CL) Culver Pictures Inc.; **123** (C) *Children on the Beach,* oil on canvas (1884), Mary Cassatt, National Gallery of Art, Washington, D.C./age fotostock/SuperStock, (C) Getty Images; **124** (C, CL) ©Musée Marmottan, Paris, France/Giraudon/Bridgeman Art Library; **125** *The Japanese Bridge,* Giverny, 1892 (oil on canvas), Claude Monet/©Private Collection/Bridgeman Art Library; **126** (CL) ©Thinkstock, (CR) ©Hulton-Deutsch Collection/Corbis; **127** (C) ©Christie's Images/Bridgeman Art Library, (TC) Getty Images; **128** (CL) ©age fotostock/SuperStock, (CR) Courtesy of the Cammie G. Henry Research Center, Watson Memorial Libary, Northwestern State University of Louisiana; **129** (C) *The Wash,* 1950s, painting by Clementine Hunter. Oil on board, 18 by 24 in. The Ethel Morrison Van Derlip Fund/The Minneapolis Institute of Arts, (TC) Getty Images